Stokesay Castle

Henry Summerson

Introduction

Settled on gently rising ground in the valley of the river Onny, Stokesay Castle seems a permanent feature of the landscape. Although there were earlier structures on the site, almost everything visible at Stokesay today was built in the 1280s and early 1290s by Laurence of Ludlow, a wool merchant who had become one of the richest men in England.

The impression of placidity and permanence was probably always intended, meaning to show that Laurence had become a member of England's landowning class, without suggesting that his arrival constituted any kind of threat, either to the great and long-established lords of the Anglo-Welsh marches, or to passers-by on the road from Ludlow to Shrewsbury.

Its military appearance was superficial. It could not have withstood a serious siege, as the expansive windows on both sides of the hall make clear, and although from the road the south tower might look like a gatehouse, it contained no passageway from which marauders could swoop down on travellers – the real gatehouse was on the other side of the castle.

Yet the walls and moat were not entirely ornamental. Laurence's wealth needed protection, and the defences were at least strong enough to resist the attempts of robbers. Stokesay was designed to provide its owner with status and security, but to do so with an air of restraint, even modesty – an air that subsequent owners have been careful to preserve.

Above: Frances Stackhouse Acton (1794–1881), who recognized the rare worth of Stokesay Castle, and in 1853 persuaded the then owner, Lord Craven, to prevent it falling into ruin

Facing page: Stokesay Castle from the north-west, looking towards the solar block and the south tower

Tour

The visitor to Stokesay Castle sees the peaceful side of the Middle Ages. Its surrounding walls have gone, and nearly everything visible today has a domestic, not a military, character. The courtyard is dominated by the 13th-century great hall, where the lord and his household ate, and by two towers whose spacious rooms were designed more for comfort than protection. The only important later addition, the charming mid-17th-century gatehouse, did nothing to make the site more defensible; Stokesay Castle still delights the eye as it was surely always intended to do.

FOLLOWING THE TOUR

The numbers beside the headings highlight key points on the tour, and correspond with the small numbered plans in the margins.

▌ THE GATEHOUSE

Much of the charm of Stokesay Castle lies in its gatehouse, built in 1640–41. Nothing is known of the original gatehouse, which was probably stone and intended to show a serious face to anyone approaching it. The present gatehouse, with its elaborately carved brackets and lozenge patterns, has many parallels among 17th-century houses in Ludlow.

At ground level its walls are close-studded (made of upright timbers in-filled with plaster). The storey above is jettied out over the ground floor. On the outer side two rows of four square panels, each containing a lozenge, flank the window over the gate-passage. A gable above has a central window with a star on each side of it, a row of five stars beneath it, and a pattern of quarter circles above.

The biblical story of the fall of man is carved along the lintel above the entrance, with the trees of life and of the knowledge of good and evil at each end, and Adam, the serpent, and Eve between them. Adam and Eve appear again on the brackets flanking the entrance, while the brackets to the south are carved as acanthus leaves and those to the north as a pair of dragons. Angels top the wooden pilasters set on either side of the window above.

The inner side of the gatehouse repeats the exterior design, with the addition of two doors, but the carving is even more flamboyant. Dragons grasp a shield over the doorway and on the brackets on either side are a man and a woman in Jacobean dress, accompanied respectively by a nude woman, half-hidden, and a nude man. More human figures support the low arches beneath the window above.

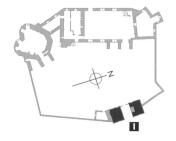

Below and bottom: Detail of the spyhole in the wicket gate that is set within the nail-studded main gate of the 17th-century gatehouse (main picture)

Facing page: A detail of the ornately carved overmantel in the solar

2 THE COURTYARD AND ITS BUILDINGS

Shortly after the present gatehouse was built, in 1640–41, the Civil War led to the curtain wall's being largely demolished. Before then there were probably storerooms along these walls, and a protective cover over the well to keep dust and dirt out of the water. A kitchen building, perhaps with a bakehouse attached, abutted the east wall of the north tower (there is no trace of an internal kitchen anywhere in the castle), until it was demolished in about 1800.

The symmetry of the buildings along the west side of the courtyard is noteworthy, especially when later changes are

RECONSTRUCTION
OF STOKESAY CASTLE
IN ABOUT 1290

taken into account. The profile of the roof of the north tower matches that of the solar block at the other end of the hall. The east face of the hall is broken by four high pointed gables, three of which contain full-length twin lancets (high, narrow windows ending in pointed arches) with a circular light above. The fourth, which is pierced below by the door into the hall, originally also had above it a half-length window (now blocked up), a combination matched in the east face of the solar block. The local stone of these exteriors was probably once covered with plaster, as the interior of the hall certainly was.

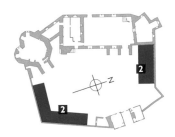

Facing page: The well, solar block and south tower as they stand now. Two wood-framed buildings that once stood in front of the solar block were demolished, probably in the late 18th or early 19th century (see the watercolour on page 29)

KEY

1 South tower

2 Solar block

3 Pentice and walkway

4 Hall

5 North tower

6 Kitchen

7 Well

8 Storerooms (probable)

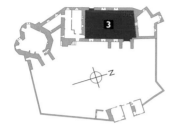

⬛ THE HALL

A visitor to Stokesay in the early 1290s would surely have been struck by its owner's wealth and taste even before he entered one of the buildings, but the wide open space of the hall must have been particularly impressive, all the more so for being clearly lit.

Three large windows on the east side are matched on the west, and the smaller (blocked-up) window over the entrance has its counterpart in the one over the stair. The southernmost window on the west side was replaced by a doorway when the hall was used as a store in the 19th century. As was usual in the 13th century, only the upper parts of the windows were glazed, the lower levels were open to the elements in fine weather and covered by wooden shutters in cold or rain.

In the 13th century, as today, the visitor's eye must have turned first to the roof, to the splendid cruck timbers covering the whole expanse of the hall.

Construction of the Hall Roof

The three great wooden arches over the hall are a rare survival for this period. Each is supported by two horizontal collars. The topmost collars are supported below by pairs of struts, but the lower collars have arched braces whose curves moderate the straight lines and vertical pull of the roof. The arches are linked by purlins (horizontal beams) running along the side walls of the roof, but, daringly, there are no

Below: Carpenters constructing a roof, from a manuscript dating from about 1315 to 1320

vertical king-posts to provide extra stability. Originally the crucks came down almost to ground level, to the corbels that can still be seen set into the walls, but their lower levels became so rotten that in the 19th century they were replaced by stone pilasters.

There is no evidence that the hall ever had aisles – a cruck roof made them unnecessary by transferring the weight of the roof to the walls – but there would have been a screen across it, probably between the doorway and the first pair of windows at the north end. This would have reduced the size of the hall when it was used for its principal function, that of providing an eating space for the household.

Above: The great hall today. Remains of the original plasterwork can be seen on the north and south walls

KEY TO THE HALL ROOF

1 Collar
2 Strut
3 Brace
4 Purlin
5 Cruck
6 Corbel
7 Pilaster

Above: Watercolour by Frances Stackhouse Acton, showing the hall in the early 19th century, when it was used for storage and barrel-making

Below: In this early 14th-century manuscript servants prepare food and carry it through to be eaten, much as they would have done when Laurence lived at Stokesay

It is not known where Laurence obtained his timber, but a few years after his death his eldest son William was recorded as buying 24 oaks from the royal woods at Bushmoor and Haycrust, about five miles north of Stokesay. The trees were cut up where they fell, under the supervision of a carpenter who marked the beams and planks for reassembly.

The same marks of arcs and circles are found in the north tower, hall and solar block, and show that all these buildings were erected at the same time and probably overseen by the same carpenter. The timbers have been dated by dendrochronology (tree-ring dating) to the late 1280s.

The Hall in Use

We can imagine Laurence, his family and guests, in about 1290, entering the hall through the south-east door and sitting at a table set across it between the first pair of full-length windows. Down the hall stretched tables for servants and manorial officers – two tables with seating for five or six men on each side would imply the presence of 20 to 25 people, the same sized household as that of a well-to-do knight. The main table was probably raised above floor level by a dais and a fire would have burned in front of it on the octagonal stone hearth. The smoke escaped through an opening in the roof (traces of smoke can be seen up among the roof timbers). A screen placed across the hall would have excluded draughts from doors and windows.

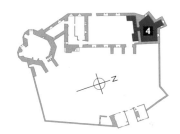

The servants may have slept in the hall or in one of the buildings that once stood in the courtyard. In the 17th century, as may have been the case in Laurence's time, there were beds in a room over the kitchen warmed by the heat rising from below. The kitchen has vanished, but the door in the hall's north wall leads down into what was probably the buttery, where ale and wine were stored in butts, or casks. It forms the basement of the castle's north tower and may originally have provided lodgings, most likely for guests; clear traces of floral decoration can be seen on the remaining plasterwork, perhaps dating from about 1300.

The rectangular projection at the north end (whose windows retain two wooden shutters) contains a pit that may once have been an ice-house used to preserve meat. The odds and ends excavated from it (some of these are on display on the top floor) suggest that it later served as a scullery where dishes were cleaned, and occasionally broken.

4 THE STAIRCASE AND THE NORTH TOWER

The two upper floors of the north tower are reached from the hall via one of its most striking features, a wooden staircase. There is an excellent view of the hall roof from the top landing. Like the roof, the staircase is a survival from the late 13th century and the same carpenters' marks occur on both.

Below: Traces of the floral decoration on the remaining plasterwork of the buttery
***Bottom:** The view from below the salt. A lord dines with his family and friends, in an early 14th-century illustration. A hanging decorates the wall behind them*

Right: The hall looking towards the
staircase at the north end, showing
the doorways to the buttery at
ground level, the first floor and the
second floor off the top landing
Below: Detail of the 13th-century
tiles on the first floor of the north
tower. Decorated earthenware
floor-tiles were produced throughout
England, but were expensive, and
usually found only in castles and
large religious establishments

Facing page: Stokesay Castle looking
across the pond, from the west

Laurence's buildings were lavish in their use of high quality
wood. The treads of the staircase are cut from whole
tree-trunks. The handrail of the short section leading to the
first floor is a later replacement, but the sturdy brackets
supporting the landing have been there since the 1290s,
together with the oak treads and the upper portion of the
handrail, moulded to provide a grip.

Wooden panels were once fitted into the now empty
spaces between the banisters – the grooves into which they
fitted can be seen, and felt, on the underside of the original
part of the handrail.

The First Floor

At the top of the first flight of stairs, a doorway of characteristic
late 13th-century design gives access to the north tower's
first floor. Although now two rooms, originally the whole floor
seems to have been occupied by one large room.

To the west of the present dividing wall are flagstones and
to the east decorative tiles that may have been brought to
Stokesay from Laurence's family home in Ludlow, where very
similar tiles have been found in excavations. In the north wall
overlooking the tiles is a 13th-century window, noticeably
larger than the lancets otherwise found at this level. These
differences in detail, together with the addition of a fireplace,
suggest that the division of the single room dates back almost
to the time of the original construction.

The first partition was probably made of wood, but in
the 17th century this was replaced by the existing wall. At the
same time the closet at the north end, set above the ice-house

Above: The second-floor room in the north tower, with its truss roof and partitioned-off corner (presumably a closet)

Below: The fireplace of the second-floor room, set in the south wall and retaining its 13th-century wooden mantel and carved surround

or scullery in the basement, was created as a latrine with a door and a wood-and-lath partition to provide privacy and exclude smells.

The Second Floor

This room has a fine wooden roof, simpler than that of the hall, with the overhead rafters resting on a truss (a supportive framework) of diagonal beams and vertical king-posts supported by horizontal tie-beams. The present roof is made of 19th-century timber, but was modelled on what was there before. Not everything in this room has remained faithful to its medieval origins, however.

During the 17th century a plaster ceiling concealed the roof timbers, and what seems to have been a closet was inserted in its north-west corner – no doubt the gaps between the timbers were boarded over. The windows, too, with their glass lozenges, are typical of the 17th century, as are the upright ovolos (curved, convex mouldings) of their frames.

But overall the top floor has retained its original shape, not least in being larger than the room beneath it, thanks to an overhanging floor, which is jettied out on three sides and supported by wooden brackets resting on stone corbels (projecting supports, which can be seen from outside).

In the south wall the elegant fireplace again displays the high quality of Laurence's house. The semicircular columns with their carved corbels and capitals and the wooden mantel that rests upon them are all of the late 13th century. All that is missing is the hood, probably of plaster, which was once placed on the mantel and fastened to the wall above, to lead the smoke up through the chimney-flue.

The Manor of Stokesay

A number of court rolls and financial accounts from between the late 14th and early 16th centuries survive from Stokesay. They show how the castle was both a lord's residence and the centre of a working farm, where the demesnes – the lands managed by the lord – supported both crops (wheat and oats are recorded) and livestock, notably cattle, sheep and pigs. Skins and wool were usually sold, but the meat helped to feed the household, as did the produce of a dovecote and orchards. The needs of fast-days and Lent were largely met by a fishery in the river Onny.

Lordship gave the Ludlows control of many aspects of their tenants' lives. The peasants of Stokesay were required to take their corn to be ground at their lord's mill, and they also had to attend his court, where they could be fined for minor offences. Some of them were still serfs, obliged to work their lord's demesnes at certain times. The profits of the estate went into buying more livestock, for both the farm and the larder, and also into buying necessities such as candles, salt, wine, spare parts for ploughs, and metal for the maintenance of buildings. In the years around 1420 lead and iron were bought for repairs to a granary, a stable and one of the towers.

William Ludlow fought in France in the king's army and his return in 1422 or 1423 may have been unexpected at Stokesay, since food had to be bought for him and only cheese and eggs could be found. Most of the recorded payments were of this severely practical kind. But when William's wife, Isabel, had a baby in 1424, her proud husband paid 3s. 4d. to three minstrels, so that the joyful occasion could be celebrated with music.

When Isabel Ludlow had a baby in 1424, her proud husband paid 3s. 4d. to three minstrels, so that the joyful occasion could be celebrated with music

Above: Three musicians depicted in a French manuscript of the mid-15th century

Left: Much of the Ludlows' income came from rents, augmented by manorial rights. In this French manuscript of about 1490 a lord of a manor receives his dues while in the background a clerk does the paperwork

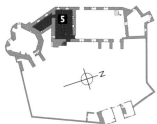

5 THE SOLAR BLOCK

At the other end of the hall stands the two-storey solar block. Laurence probably used this for his own living quarters before he built the south tower.

The Ground Floor

The door in the hall's south-east wall gives access to the ground floor, which was originally a large single room with a cellar reached down a flight of stairs. It was probably used mainly as a storeroom, a function emphasized by its 17th-century adaptation that divided the room down the middle and set panelling and cupboards in the wall behind the hall. Perhaps at some point it became a dining room, with food from an outside kitchen and drink from the cellar passed through the hatch cut in the dividing wall.

The room's medieval origin can be seen in the window in the west wall, one of the two which lit the original room. Though it overlooks the moat, a grille provided extra security. In the room on the other side of the dividing wall is another medieval window. Next to it a doorway leads into a passageway that ends in a wall. Lit only by two small windows (one of

them little more than a slit), protected by the moat below, and set directly beneath his own dwelling at the farthest point in the castle from its entrance, this was probably Laurence's strong room – a secure repository for money and perhaps wool.

The Solar

The solar is reached by going outside and up the flight of steps immediately to the right of the door. These are modern, but replaced a medieval stairway – the line of the sloping roof, or pentice, that sheltered people passing between the solar and the hall is clearly visible in the wall immediately below the solar's truncated window. The door at the top of the stairs leads into the solar, originally private apartments for Laurence and his family.

Like many other rooms in the castle, but more extensively than most, the solar was refashioned in the 17th century, probably about the time that the gatehouse was replaced. The ceiling dates from that time, as do the ornately carved overmantel, the cornices above and below it, and the panelling round the walls. The overmantel is divided by pilasters shaped as human figures into four squares, two of which have a

Top: An early 19th-century watercolour showing the solar being used as a granary – a use observed by the antiquarian John Britton when he visited in 1813. By this time the panelling and overmantel had clearly lost the coloured paintwork with which they were originally decorated

Above: Early 19th-century watercolour, possibly by the same artist, showing the blocked-up windows of the solar, probably shortly after the demolition of the two buildings that had stood in front of them (see page 29)

Facing page: The solar today

Above: A photograph taken in about 1900 showing the wall af the solar block with its windows covered with ivy

Below: A painted Tudor rose, now concealed by the panelling that surrounds the west window of the solar

grotesque head at their centre. It was originally brightly coloured (traces of several different pigments can be seen on it) and may have been carved from a Flemish design. Cornices were needed to cover portions of wall that were left exposed after the overmantel had been put up, suggesting it was not made specifically for its present position.

The 17th-century designer mostly respected the room's medieval outline. Although the new ceiling hid the openwork roofing from sight it was left undisturbed. The fireplace stands where its predecessor stood. The panelling carefully framed the peepholes on either side of the fireplace, through which earlier owners could observe what was happening in the hall, and although it covered some 16th-century paintwork, it left untouched the windows and window-seat in the west wall. The only significant change inside the room was in the east wall, where the original window was blocked up.

The medieval window has since been reopened but a picture of about 1900 shows the wall and blocked-up window covered with ivy. The view from the original window may have been obscured by new buildings outside, for a rectangular window was cut in the wall beside it.

Another change involved the creation of an extension. The door in the south-west corner of the solar block originally led onto a walkway above the putative strong room below (perhaps to enable a man to keep guard over it). Probably in the early 17th century the curtain wall was raised here, allowing another room to be built on top of the lower one. It has a pointed roof and latrine, and may have been intended for a guest-room, or simply an additional amenity for its lord or tenant.

6 THE SOUTH TOWER

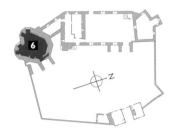

When the solar block was built in the 1280s it was the southernmost part of the west wall complex. A window in its south wall, next to the entrance, would have provided a view over open ground in the direction of the road. Today it looks straight into the solid masonry of the south tower, which was begun shortly afterwards.

Laurence may have built the additional tower so that he could leave the solar block and north tower for his children (he and his wife Agnes had at least six). But it is more likely that as he became richer and more important – an adviser and moneylender to the king and to the magnates of the Welsh marches – it was built as an appropriate demonstration of his growing status. Here he could direct his ever-expanding business and receive people who came to borrow the money that commercial success brought him.

The tower was clearly intended to provide its owner with protection as well as showing off his architectural taste. Although its entrance was not defended by a drawbridge, as was once thought (the lead-filled holes over the door did not hold ropes or chains, but supported a porch), it could still provide a secure residence. The walls may have many windows, but they are thick enough to contain stairways. The tower's original timbers were mostly destroyed by a fire in 1830 (some wooden shutters survived), but the present floors appear to be where their predecessors were.

The First Floor

The first floor is occupied by a single room lit by windows almost all the way round. Two are lancets, but four are large enough to contain seats. On a sunny day, with views in most

Below: The first-floor room of the south tower, with its 17th-century fireplace. The recess between the windows may have been used to stand lamps in at night-time or when the shutters were closed

Above: The south tower, from the south beyond the moat

Below: On the second floor above the entrance of the south tower is a double window that may once have been a door, providing access to a balcony or enabling the delivery or removal of large items of furniture

directions, this must have been a pleasant place to sit. As there are no grooves in the windows to hold glass, the shutters would have been closed in bad weather and warmth provided by the fire in the east wall. The existing fireplace is 17th century, but since its flue leads to a medieval chimney it must have replaced an earlier hearth in the same position. A latrine was reached down a passage to the right of the fireplace. Two recesses in the walls may have held lamps to provide light when the shutters were closed.

The Second Floor

A straight stair cut in the wall to the right of the entrance leads up to the second floor. It has another latrine at its head, next to the door into the adjoining room. Before the fire in 1830 this room was reportedly divided into three by wooden partitions, but originally it probably formed a single room like the one beneath, with two windows looking into the courtyard and others facing south, and a fireplace in the east wall to provide warmth.

One of the windows, almost over the entrance to the tower, consists of two small rectangular lights, and from the outside looks more like a door than a window. It may have provided access to a wooden balcony, or served as a point from which beds and other heavy items of furniture, too bulky to be brought in up the narrow stairs, were hauled up to the second storey.

The Roof

Next to the window another stair in the wall leads to the roof. This is now flat and made of lead covered by wooden slats, but once it was occupied by a small shed-like structure with a pointed wooden roof, perhaps for use by sentries during the Civil War. The battlements still have many of the hinges and fastenings to which, if the castle were attacked, boards would have been attached across the openings to protect anyone standing on top of the tower. Defenders could have fired through slits in the battlements.

A turret on the north side of the tower provided an observation point, as indeed the whole roof still does – there are fine views in all directions. To the west is a pond that dates from the same period as the tower. Like the castle, the pond was both ornamental and practical. It enhanced the view of the castle from the west but also provided an extra element of protection, acted as a potential water supply for the moat, and no doubt also contained fish.

The Basement

Back at ground level, there is a basement that now can only be entered from outside, but which originally could also be reached by a stair from behind the first-floor entrance to the tower. The external entrance to the basement, set between two large buttresses of uncertain date, was a double doorway, with one door where the present one is, and another on the other side of the space where the internal stairway ends.

Above: One of the twin-lighted windows in the south tower basement, overlooking the moat
Below: Watercolour by an unknown artist showing the basement of the south tower in use as a smithy in the early 19th century. One of the twin-lighted windows can be seen on the far side of the room

Over the doorway is a lancet, enabling occupants to keep an eye on anyone approaching the tower. There is no medieval fireplace – the present one dates from the 18th century, when the basement acted as a smithy – and no latrine, which suggests that the basement was intended to provide protection for money and goods rather than accommodation for people. Positioned directly beneath the lord's apartment, to which it was linked by the internal stair, it may well have been his new strong room, replacing the likely one off the solar block. It has four windows, two of them with twin lights, but these are all set over the moat and were doubtless given added protection by grilles or shutters.

■7 THE EXTERIOR OF THE CASTLE

Encircling the castle is the moat, which can be entered from in front of the gatehouse. It is not clear whether it was filled with water in the 13th century. A 1731 engraving by Samuel and Nathaniel Buck depicts the moat filled with water but there is no sign now of a water-retaining clay lining to the banks. Even when dry the moat would have been a formidable barrier to robbers and raiders, as the curtain walls would have been when they stood to their full height. The stub of wall on the east side of the south tower makes this very clear.

Inside the courtyard all that can be seen of the south tower are five sides of an apparent octagon, a conventional enough design. But seen from outside its remarkable design becomes apparent: on its south side the remaining three sides are replaced by two five-sided projecting lobes with a space between them. From a distance the effect is that of a twin-towered battlemented gatehouse, like those that Edward I (r.1272–1307) was building in Wales at castles such as Rhuddlan and Harlech, but smaller.

Below: The first suggestion that the moat at Stokesay once held water dates only from 1731. An engraving by Samuel and Nathaniel Buck, which does not seem to be always accurate on points of detail, depicts the moat as filled by a stream running from ponds on the castle's west side

▣ THE CHURCH OF ST JOHN THE BAPTIST

This simple church consists of a nave and chancel with a tower at the west end. In its oldest parts, notably its Norman south door, it pre-dates the castle, but it was largely rebuilt after damage done during the Civil War.

The interior is a rare example of an Anglican church that has retained mid-17th-century fittings. Its woodwork, dating from almost exactly the same time as the refurbishment of the castle by the Baldwyns, who occupied Stokesay during part of the 17th century and into the 18th, further illustrates the quality of craftsmanship available in Shropshire at the time.

The post-Reformation church emphasized the word rather than the image, hence the light whitewashed walls interrupted only by monuments and two panels painted with the Ten Commandments beside the gallery at the west end of the nave. Attention was focused less on the altar than on the pulpit, which was originally a triple-decker but later reduced in height. Wooden pews accommodated the parishioners. Five small ones under the gallery escaped destruction in the 1640s, the rest, larger and of superior workmanship, date from the church's restoration that began in the mid-1650s, as do the handsome canopied pews at the east end of the nave. No doubt these were where the Baldwyns sat, where they could look directly across at the preacher.

Until the middle of the 19th century congregational singing was accompanied by a small band of musicians seated in the gallery. They were superseded by a harmonium, which was subsequently replaced by the present organ.

Above: The view from the top of the south tower over the roof of the great hall, towards the church of St John the Baptist beyond

Below: The twin-towered battlemented gatehouse of Rhuddlan Castle in Wales, built by Edward I between 1277 and 1282. From a distance the south tower of Stokesay Castle gives a similar, though less imposing, effect

History

Stokesay Castle was
built in the late 1280s
by a local merchant,
Laurence of Ludlow,
using his vast profits
from the wool trade.
Laurence's descendants
and their successors
lived mostly quiet lives
at Stokesay for some
350 years. One of them,
William, Lord Craven,
built the delightful
gatehouse, shortly
before the castle walls
were demolished during
the Civil War of the
1640s. During the 18th
century the buildings
were allowed to decay,
until in the 1870s the
glovemaker John Derby
Allcroft restored them,
and saved the castle
for posterity.

Left: Life in medieval Shropshire was under constant threat of war as the Anglo-Saxons, Welsh and Normans fought for land. In this 12th-century manuscript Gerald of Wales depicts the violent tendencies of England's Celtic neighbours

Below: A man catching bees, from an early 14th-century manuscript. The manor of Stokesay is first mentioned in Domesday Book of 1086: 'There is a mill paying nine quarters of corn, and a miller there, and a keeper of bees'

Facing page: The future Edward I (right) and his companions prepare to leave on crusade in August 1270. John de Verdon, lord of Stokesay, went with them

EARLY HISTORY

For centuries medieval Shropshire lay under the shadow of violence and war, as first Anglo-Saxons and Welsh fought for supremacy, and then after 1066 aggressive Norman kings and lords endeavoured to impose themselves on both.

Nothing is known of Stokesay until Domesday Book was compiled in 1086. At that time it formed part of a prosperous estate called simply 'Stoches' – an Anglo-Saxon word suggesting the presence of a cattle-farm. It was held by the Lacys, originally from Lassy in Normandy, who became lords of Weobley and Ludlow and one of the great families of the Welsh marches.

'Stoches' was soon divided into two manors, North and South Stoke. During the reign of Henry I (r. 1100–35) the latter was entrusted to Theodoric de Say, also of Norman origin, whose descendants held it as tenants of the Lacys for over a century and gave it their name (North Stoke became Stoke upon Tern). Closely related to the early lords of Clun, due west of Stokesay, the Says were important people in the Welsh marches and, like the Lacys, also had interests in Ireland. When Walter de Lacy died in 1241, leaving only two granddaughters as his heirs, Hugh de Say made a deal with John de Verdon (c. 1226–74), the husband of one of them, giving Stokesay to John in return for Irish estates.

In the late 1250s and early 1260s Verdon was prominent among Henry III's supporters against Simon de Montfort, earl of Leicester and leader of the opposition to the king during the barons' war. Verdon may have made Stokesay his base in this time of hostilities – a dendrochronological survey has dated timbers in the solar block to the years 1261–63. But in May 1264 he was taken prisoner with Henry III and his son Prince Edward at Lewes, and once the civil wars were over he went on crusade, leaving Stokesay in the hands of a tenant who, in 1281, sold his rights in the manor to a completely new sort of lord, the Shropshire wool merchant Laurence of Ludlow.

Above: Shepherds with their sheep depicted in an illustration of the Nativity of about 1325. Sheep were a valuable commodity at this time. An experienced shepherd was therefore a respected, and relatively highly paid, figure in his community

LAURENCE OF LUDLOW AND STOKESAY

How much Laurence gave for Stokesay is unrecorded. In 1270 the manor was reckoned to be worth £26 13s. 4d. per annum to its owner; if Laurence paid at the usual rate of ten years' purchase then it will have cost him £266, a substantial sum, but well within the means of a man who could afford to lend John Lestrange, lord of Knockin, £4,000 in a single transaction.

Laurence had inherited, and then expanded, a flourishing business from his father Nicholas, selling the fine wools of the Welsh marches in England and abroad. The profits enabled him to lend money to many of the great lords of the march, men such as Richard Fitzalan, earl of Arundel and lord of Clun, and Edmund Mortimer, lord of Wigmore. They also enabled him to buy property. He is one of the earliest known examples of a rich townsman who set up as a country squire.

Landownership brought status in medieval England, status that a fine house enhanced. The dendrochronological evidence shows that building at Stokesay began no earlier than 1285, and until it was completed Laurence appears to have continued to live in his family house in Ludlow – he recorded making a loan there in 1289. But on 19 October 1291 he obtained a royal licence to crenellate – to fortify – his house at Stokesay, probably just before he took up residence there.

Such a licence was a further mark of status, but though the completed house could not have withstood a determined siege, its fortifications were not purely ornamental. Laurence was one of the richest men in England and, in an age before

Laurence of Ludlow and the Wool Trade

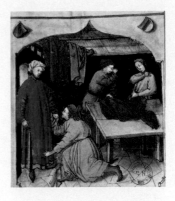

In the 13th century wool was England's most important export, and the principal source of the nation's wealth. The wool of the Welsh marches was of high quality and Laurence dealt in large quantities of it.

When he sailed from London on his last voyage, Laurence had with him some 180 sacks of his own wool; these would have contained about 46,000 fleeces, with a cash value of at least £1,200. It is nearly impossible to give modern equivalents for medieval money, but the fact that a 13th-century ploughman could expect to earn about 35s. a year may give some idea of the scale of Laurence's earnings from the sale of wool.

Laurence and his agents negotiated with local magnates, monasteries, the lords of single manors, and groups of farmers, buying up their wool clips in advance and taking possession of them after shearing time. Although much of his business would have been done from Shrewsbury, Laurence seems also to have had an office in London (it was there that he lent 100 marks – £66 13s. 4d. – to Worcester Priory in 1292), and he is known to have attended Boston Fair in Lincolnshire, which was a major gathering-place for foreign merchants. But he also went overseas in pursuit of business. He sold wool in person to merchants in the Low Countries, where it fed the cloth industry of towns such as Ghent, Bruges and Ypres, and he attended at least one of the fairs of Champagne, in north-west France, which acted as meeting places for merchants from all over Europe.

Laurence may have used his profits to buy goods to sell in England; he certainly brought some of his gains home in the form of foreign currency, which he then exchanged for sterling at the royal mint. A single transaction in 1289 brought him nearly £440. His enterprises at home and abroad made him an outstandingly rich man.

When Laurence sailed from London on his last voyage he had with him some 180 sacks of his own wool, containing about 46,000 fleeces

Above: A mid-15th-century depiction of a shop selling woollen cloth. A merchant prepares to cut cloth to fit a customer while another displays the wares

Left: A woman spinning wool is interrupted by an amorous man (about 1325)

Above: A map of the area surrounding Stokesay. The proximity of the castle to both Ludlow and Shrewsbury was ideal for business
Below: A shipwreck, drawn by the 13th-century St Albans monk Matthew Paris. The chronicler of Dunstable Priory, whose own monastery was hit by the increase in customs duty, recorded Laurence's death with undisguised satisfaction: 'because he sinned against the wool-growers, he was swallowed by the waves in a ship full of wool'

banks, doubtless kept much of his ready cash at home. That and his likely possession of fine clothes, furnishings, plate and jewellery, could easily have made him a target for the criminal bands that haunted the roads in late 13th-century England. Hence the stone curtain walls enclosing Stokesay Castle, and features such as the double door that barred access to the south tower's basement.

Laurence did not abandon the wool trade when he bought Stokesay, which was almost certainly intended to be a commercial asset rather than a retirement home. It enabled him to diversify his interests by providing him with land on which to rear sheep; by 1292 he was selling cloth in Ludlow, probably made from home-grown wool.

More importantly, Stokesay was ideally placed for business purposes. It was situated on the main road that ran from Shrewsbury (which seems to have been his commercial base) to Ludlow, where his family originated, and from there to London and the south. Moreover it provided easy access to the valley of the river Onny where it turns west towards Montgomery and central Wales.

During his lifetime Laurence was the most important wool merchant in England, so much so that in 1294 not only did he lend more than £600 to King Edward I but he also advised him about commercial policy. It was at his suggestion that Edward, desperate for money to finance a war with France, tripled the customs rate on wool exports, from one mark (13s. 4d.) to £2 per sack.

Other wool-producers were outraged, and could not conceal their delight when the fleet carrying wool, money and Laurence of Ludlow ran into a storm on the night of 26 November. Most of the ships and wool survived, but Laurence was drowned off the Suffolk coast. His body was recovered and brought back to Ludlow for burial.

Left: An early 19th-century watercolour by an unknown artist, showing the covered well and the buildings that used to adjoin the solar block
Below: Henry V (r. 1413–22), under whom William Ludlow fought in France during the 1420s in the aftermath of the battle of Agincourt

THE LATER LUDLOWS, 1294–1498

Whether or not Laurence ever expected his children to live at Stokesay, it was probably to provide for them that he bought a good deal of property in Shropshire in the 1280s and early 1290s. So successfully did his descendants put down roots that they remained lords of Stokesay for more than two centuries. None of them engaged in trade, rather they became members of the county's ruling class, taking their wives from other landowning families and repeatedly acting as sheriffs, JPs and members of parliament.

Occasionally their seemingly quiet lives were disturbed by outbreaks of violence. Laurence of Ludlow's grandson and namesake, the founder of Ludlow's Carmelite friary, appears to have been killed in an affray in 1353, some ten years after his brother William had met a similar end. Late in the 14th century Sir Richard Ludlow (d. 1390) was reported to have put the fear of death into the parson of Wistanstow, a man whose name – Edmund Ludlow – suggests that he was Sir Richard's close relation, perhaps even his brother. In the early 1420s another William Ludlow engaged in a different sort of violence, serving under Henry V in France. But more often the Ludlows kept out of dangerous occupations and devoted themselves to running their estates and promoting family interests.

As often happened in the Middle Ages, it was not involvement in civil or foreign wars that brought a landed family to extinction, but simply a lack of male heirs. When another Sir Richard Ludlow died on 23 December 1498 he had been predeceased by his son and grandson, and his heirs were his two granddaughters, Anne and Alice, who had married two brothers, Thomas and Humphrey Vernon, members of an important Derbyshire family. The 16-year-old Anne's share of the Ludlow estates included Stokesay, which thus passed through her and Thomas to new owners.

Above: Reconstruction drawing of
Stokesay Castle in the mid-17th
century, soon after the new
gatehouse was built. Note the
wooden-framed buildings attached
to the solar block and the kitchen
block adjoining the north tower

THE SIXTEENTH AND EARLY SEVENTEENTH CENTURIES

In about 1543 the antiquary John Leland passed through
Shropshire, and noted that Stokesay was 'buildid like a castel'.
References to 'le Castill diche' in 15th-century accounts
suggest that it was already being referred to locally as a castle
by then, but the title 'Stokesay Castle' only starts to become
common in the 16th and 17th centuries. This perhaps reflects
the social pretensions of its owners, and particularly of Henry
Vernon (1548–1606), who succeeded his grandfather Thomas
in 1563 and thereafter devoted most of his energies, and
money, to an obsessive pursuit of the lands and title of the
barony of Powys.

An endless series of lawsuits meant that Henry spent
much of his time in London, but he returned to Stokesay
at intervals, most likely to raise money from his estates. He
sometimes received guests there, as when he bought fish,
bread and wine to entertain a Mrs Bingham (probably the
wife of one of his creditors) in 1583, and is twice recorded
as doing business in 'the paved chamber', probably the room
with the flagstoned floor in the north tower. Perhaps that
tower was his preferred residence in the castle, since he had
repairs made to its top floor in about 1577. He also attended
services in the nearby parish church, for instance on 4 March
1576, when he gave 6d. to a poor man there.

Henry Vernon failed to become a peer. In order to
discredit a deed of conveyance drawn up by the last Lord

Powys he had concocted a bizarre story that it had been forged posthumously by conspirators who had opened the dead man's coffin, put a pen in the corpse's hand and with it traced his signature on the document. Henry Vernon haunted the courts for decades with this tale, ignoring the hostility of Queen Elizabeth and brushing aside moments of farce, like the discovery that vital documents had been nibbled into illegibility by mice. For many years Vernon lived lavishly, on borrowed money according to his enemies. He bought fine clothes, for instance in 1576, when he paid for 'a white canvas doublet wavy laid with white silk lace' and 'a new taffeta hat with a bugle band and a black sprig in it'. He also bought a brush for his beard, and in February 1583 spent 2*d.* on 'potata roots'.

It was not, however, extravagance that effectively ruined him, but his standing surety for the debt of another man who defaulted. By the end of 1591 he was in the Fleet Prison. He was released in 1592 but his fortunes never recovered. Overwhelmed by debts, he sold Stokesay to Sir George Mainwaring (d. 1628) for £6,000 in 1598, but in 1606 he died in rented lodgings in Stoke Newington.

Mainwaring did not keep Stokesay for long, however, and in 1620 it was bought, with other Shropshire properties, by the immensely rich widow of a former Lord Mayor of London, Dame Elizabeth Craven (d. 1624), and her young son William for a total of £13,500.

Early 17th-century Stokesay was a valuable estate, surrounded by woods and supporting horses, sheep and cattle. By the 1640s it was worth over £300 per annum.

Above: Elizabethan finery, as worn by Robert Devereux, second earl of Essex and favourite of Elizabeth I. Henry Vernon seems to have hoped to cut a similar dash

Below: A mayoress of London and her attendants, from a manuscript of about 1618. Dame Elizabeth Craven would have appeared thus in the procession of her husband, Sir William Craven, who was mayor in 1610/11

Right: William Craven (c. 1608–97), first earl of Craven, was rich, brave and cultivated. An enthusiastic soldier as a young man, his financial support for the royalists in the Civil War caused his estates to be confiscated. Having recovered them at the Restoration of Charles II, he built a number of fine houses in an up-to-date style, and also became well known for his efforts to prevent fires in London. Not everyone took him seriously, however; for Samuel Pepys he was 'that Coxcombe my lord Craven'

Below: *The title page from a contemporary account of the taking of Stokesay Castle in 1645*

William Craven (c. 1608–97) was by then an enthusiastic soldier who spent much time abroad, but he visited Stokesay in 1633, and in 1640–41 he made a permanent alteration to its appearance.

His accounts for 1640 record that during that year he spent £468 18s. 9½d. 'about the building at Stokesay', with a further £65 3s. 'for finishing the work' in the first three months of 1641. This documentary record coincides so exactly with the findings of a dendrochronological survey, which dates the timbers of the gatehouse to the years 1639–41, that it seems impossible to doubt that the accounts refer to the building of the gatehouse.

THE CIVIL WAR AND AFTER

The obviously ornamental character of the gatehouse shows that William Craven was not concerned about the defensibility of Stokesay. When civil war broke out in 1642, a year after the building of the gatehouse, he probably wondered whether he had made an error of judgement.

Shropshire was predominantly royalist, however, and it was not until 1645, and especially after parliamentary forces captured Shrewsbury on 22 February, that the county became the scene of hostilities. In June that year 800 men were sent to blockade Ludlow and, as they approached, the decision was taken to capture Stokesay, 'a garrison of the enemies … conceived considerable'.

INTELLIGENCE
FROM
SHROPSHIRE,
Of three
GREAT VICTORIES
Obtained by the Forces

of Shrewesburie

(Commanded by the Committee
there;) *viz.*

The taking of *Stokesey* and *Caus-castles*, places
of great strength; and a great Victory obtained
in the fields, with a Catalogue of the prisoners.

Sent from Persons of worth, that were in the Action,
to a Person of Honour in *London.*

Published according to Order.

LONDON,
Printed for *Thomas Underhill*, and are to be sold at
the Bible in *Woodstreet*, June 28. 1645.

Everything was done according to the conventions of 17th-century warfare. First a formal summons to surrender was sent to the garrison. Only a few months earlier the soldiers within had been complaining of 'want of clothes, shirts and shoes' and no doubt they were heavily outnumbered, but nevertheless they firmly refused to yield, as protocol required they should. The parliamentarians seemingly had no cannon with them and therefore prepared to take the castle by storm, which would have entitled them to massacre the garrison and strip the castle bare.

But again they played by the rule book, by sending a second summons to surrender. Since the defenders had by now put up the resistance expected of them, they could surrender without loss of honour and duly did so, to be replaced by a parliamentarian garrison. There is no evidence that anyone was killed, and probably not a shot was fired, though there was a fierce clash nearby a few weeks later

Left: A decidedly romanticized Victorian stained-glass picture from Stokesay Court, showing the royalist surrender of Stokesay Castle to the parliamentarians after the short siege of 1645, with all the participants apparently wearing their finest clothes

Above: An anonymous watercolour of the first floor of the south tower at the end of the 18th century, showing that the tower was panelled in the same style, and doubtless at the same time, as the main rooms in the solar block. The furniture and portraits suggest that this room was still in use, though with its bare floors, perhaps not very often

when royalists from Herefordshire tried to recapture Stokesay.

Two years later the castle's barns and stables were described as 'all pulled down' – probably they stood outside the walls and were demolished by the defenders to give themselves a clear field of fire if the need arose. A survey made in 1648 contains nothing to suggest that the castle fabric had suffered from the recent hostilities (unlike the parish church, which was severely damaged, perhaps when some royalist horsemen took refuge there in February 1646 'and stood upon their guard').

Even so, Stokesay Castle had been at serious risk, as can be seen from the payment of 5s. to a messenger 'for going to Sir William Craven when Stoke Castle was in danger of being pulled down'. Craven took no part in the fighting, but his sympathies were strongly royalist and eventually all his estates were confiscated. Meanwhile Stokesay was not pulled down, but to make it indefensible its walls were largely demolished to their present height, leaving it with no future except as a farmhouse.

Fortunately the estate was still prosperous. In October 1647 Charles Baldwyn, who was probably already its tenant, had negotiated a lease of it for three lives, explaining that 'he doth intend to make it a seat to spend the residue of his days there; and to make it commodious for such as shall enjoy it after'. Once established, Charles transferred his tenancy to his son Samuel, a rich lawyer who took up residence in the castle. His daughter Elizabeth was born there in 1650 and he was probably responsible for such domestic details as the panelling of the solar and the windows in the top room of the north tower.

In 1660 when the monarchy was restored Lord Craven recovered his lands, but although he and his heirs remained ground landlords, a series of leases kept the occupancy in the Baldwyn family. When Samuel Baldwyn died in 1683 he was succeeded by his son, another Charles. For a while the Baldwyns acted as lords of the manor. They helped to rebuild the parish church and the villagers of Stokesay showed their appreciation in traditional ways – in 1699 the churchwardens recorded a payment of 2s. 'for ringing at the birth of the lord's son'.

The younger Charles Baldwyn died in 1709 and though his descendants retained their tenancy of Stokesay almost to the end of the 18th century they ceased to live there, residing instead at Aqualate, just outside Newport. They sublet the castle to a series of tenants, at least one of whom appears to have lived there. When Thomas Tunstall, described as 'of Stoke Castle in the parish of Stokesay in the County of Salop Gentleman', drew up his will in September 1788, he directed that his widow should for the rest of her life have 'the use and enjoyment of the little parlour & the Room wherein we now sleep…'. The rooms must have been in either the south tower or the solar block, which together now formed the residential core of the castle. They were supplemented by two small structures set against the solar block's courtyard wall, covering its main window. Seemingly made of wood and plaster, they were demolished in about 1800, making it impossible to tell if they were storerooms or provided accommodation.

To an increasing extent the buildings were used as stores and workshops. When the antiquary John Britton (1771–1857) visited Stokesay in about 1813 he painted a gloomy picture of its condition: 'abandoned to neglect, and rapidly advancing to

'... abandoned to neglect, and rapidly advancing to ruin: the glass is destroyed, the ceilings and floors are falling, and the rain streams through the opening roof on the damp and mouldering walls'
The antiquarian John Britton, on Stokesay in 1813 (portrait by William Brockedon, 1831)

Below: An engraving by John Britton of 1813, the year he visited Stokesay Castle

John Derby Allcroft

John Derby Allcroft (1822–93) had a great deal in common with his distant predecessor at Stokesay, Laurence of Ludlow. Both came from the Anglo-Welsh borders and followed their fathers into trades that made their fortunes. Allcroft's business was making leather gloves, which in the 19th century were an essential accessory for every fashion-conscious woman.

From 1846 Allcroft was effectively the head of Dents, which by the mid-1880s was selling over a million pairs of gloves every year. An outstanding example of a mid-Victorian businessman, he was a frugal, industrious, yet just and generous employer. Every day he walked from his home in Lancaster Gate to his office in Cheapside and back again in the evening. He was also a committed evangelical Christian who built three London churches and gave money generously to charity.

Allcroft was clearly proud to be the owner of Stokesay Castle (a picture of it can be seen behind him in his portrait), and he had it restored with a care and restraint remarkable in an age when restoration all too often meant rebuilding. Almost nothing is known of the details of the work he financed precisely because it was so unobtrusively and sensitively done, his aim being that of 'replacing where decay was rampant, but wherever possible, leaving the original materials untouched, even in respect of their surfaces'.

Allcroft effectively retired in 1873 and, again like Laurence of Ludlow, then set up as a country gentleman, on the Stokesay estate he had bought in 1869. In 1887 he engaged the architect Thomas Harris to build him a palatial Jacobean-style residence at Stokesay Court, a few miles south-west of the castle. By 1892, when he and his family moved in, he had spent more than £100,000 on it. As well as having superb oak panelling, the new house was also one of the first in England to be fully lit by electricity.

> Allcroft was clearly proud to be the owner of Stokesay Castle (a picture of it can be seen behind him in his portrait), and he had it restored with a care and restraint remarkable in an age when restoration all too often meant rebuilding

Above: John Derby Allcroft, with the painting hanging behind him of Stokesay Castle. He built Stokesay Court to live in in his retirement but died only a year after its completion

Right: The patriarch of Stokesay Court: John Derby Allcroft surrounded by members of his household on the 'Butler's Steps' of Stokesay Court, probably in 1892, shortly before he died. With him are his daughters Harriet Jewell (back right) and Elizabeth May (bottom right), and his sons and daughters-in-law

ruin', with the hall being used for barrel-making and the solar acting as a granary. At some point the gatehouse became a refuge for a coiner and the basement of the south tower was turned into a smithy, with predictably disastrous results – a fire in 1830 burnt out all the floors.

RECOVERY AND RESTORATION

For Britton, Stokesay had been merely 'this curious specimen of an opulent country gentleman's residence in remote times'. But for Thomas Hudson Turner (1815–52), who visited in 1845, it was 'one of the most perfect and interesting 13th-century buildings which we possess'. Stokesay was not entirely neglected in the intervening period. The demolition of the old kitchen, some time before 1815, had left the hall's east wall in need of reinforcement, which was provided by the three large external buttresses that are still in position today. By the time Turner made his visit in 1845 the original wall-posts supporting the cruck roof of the hall had been replaced by convincingly medieval-looking stone pilasters. The castle was also a beneficiary of changes in outlook and taste that from the late 18th century increasingly transformed the understanding and appreciation of the Middle Ages. Among those who felt the appeal of medieval art and culture was Frances Stackhouse Acton (1794–1881), the widow of a Shropshire landowner.

'Lord Craven had it repaired, and it is now preserved with the care that [such] an example deserves'
Frances Stackhouse Acton in 1820 by H E Eridge. It was largely thanks to her efforts that she could write the above of Stokesay in 1868

Right: A party of the Allcroft family and friends having lunch in the solar in the late 19th century

Right: A party of the Allcroft family and friends having lunch in the solar in the late 19th century

'I have rarely had, for a couple of hours, the sensation of dropping back personally into the past so straight as while I lay on the grass beside the well in the little sunny court of this small castle and lazily appreciated the still definite details of medieval life'

The young Henry James (1843–1916), below, writing of his visit to Stokesay in 1877

A noted antiquarian and artist, she cared deeply about the fortunes of Stokesay Castle, and in 1853 she appealed directly to the second earl of Craven (1809–66) to take action to prevent 'by a few repairs, the destruction that surely awaits, if much longer neglected'. Her voice was heard and action followed, for only two years later the estate accounts included an outlay of £103 5s. 7d. on 'Clearing out and securing Stoke Castle'. The money was reportedly spent under Mrs Stackhouse Acton's own supervision.

Disaster had been avoided, but more would be needed to preserve the castle in the long term. In 1869 the burden was shouldered by a new owner, when John Derby Allcroft paid £215,000 for the Stokesay estate, which was described (with some chronological inaccuracy) as including 'one of the most perfect and interesting Specimens of A Fortified Mansion of the Twelfth Century Now existing, known as Stokesay Castle, situate in the centre of the property'.

Allcroft seems never to have proposed to live in the castle, but he had it carefully restored, in works that appear to have begun in about 1875, and were probably still in progress when the writer Henry James paid a visit in 1877. By then a caretaker was living in the gatehouse, and visitors had free access. Although James noted that the rooms were 'all unoccupied and in a state of extreme decay', he was enchanted by what he saw. Allcroft's work was finished by 1887 when the Woolhope Naturalists' Field Club from Herefordshire paid a visit and observed how the castle had been 'placed in a fitting state of repair'.

John Derby Allcroft died in 1893, and his descendants were no less conscientious in caring for Stokesay Castle. Thus in 1902, when urgent repairs were once more required,

A Family Visit in the 1960s

Caroline Magnus, whose uncle and aunt gave Stokesay Castle to the nation, remembers visiting the castle as a teenager:

'My earliest memory of Stokesay Castle dates from my first visit to my uncle and aunt, Philip and Jewell Magnus-Allcroft, in the late 1960s. A visit to the castle was de rigueur for all visitors to Stokesay Court. We were driven by Dick Pinches, who was my uncle's chauffeur. Philip enjoyed his afternoon drives. He sat next to Dick in the front, dressed in suit and tie, heavy overcoat and hat, and opened all the windows. I sat in the back and froze, and was delighted when Stokesay Castle turned out to be so close by.

'Before this visit I was fairly unaware of Stokesay Castle's importance, despite my family's best efforts to educate me. I was drawn to romantic tales of the wool trade and battles of the Welsh marches (not to mention Malcolm Saville's Lone Pine adventure stories, which were set in the surrounding countryside at places like Clun and Leintwardine), and a visit would provide splendid material for a powerful imagination. I recall how I climbed up onto the top of the tower – no health and safety rails then! – and imagined living in an earlier age, looking out and waiting in fear and dread for Welsh or other invaders to appear over the crest of the surrounding hills. When I learnt that Stokesay had not been built for defence, I'm ashamed to say I was rather disappointed.

'Stokesay itself could never disappoint – it is a remarkable building, and wonderfully unaltered. In those days the moat was choked with weeds, and I longed to clear it, but this sad impression was soon offset by the warm welcome I always received from the custodians, Mr and Mrs Atkins, in the tiny shop where they sold a splendid assortment of local produce, including beeswax polish and delicious honey.'

'My uncle sat next to Dick in the front, dressed in suit and tie, heavy overcoat and hat, and opened all the windows. I sat in the back and froze'

Above: *Caroline Magnus as a young woman. Caroline's aunt Jewell Magnus-Allcroft was the granddaughter of John Derby Allcroft*
Left: *The mock-Jacobean mansion, Stokesay Court, built by John Derby Allcroft, and now the home of Caroline Magnus. It was seen in cinemas in 2007 as the setting for the film Atonement*

Above: The gatehouse in 1934, with a 'banger' of the period nearby
Below: Stokesay Castle today

Herbert Allcroft took, and acted on, advice from the Society for the Protection of Ancient Buildings (SPAB). It was not goodwill on the part of the owners that was increasingly lacking as the 20th century progressed, but money, in an age of agricultural depression and rising taxes. Herbert's two children, his son, Russell, and particularly his daughter, Jewell, who had married the historian Sir Philip Magnus (who later adopted the name of Magnus-Allcroft), did their best to keep decay at bay in difficult circumstances, repeatedly turning to SPAB for advice and help. They wanted to keep Stokesay 'in the family', and long continued to spend such money as they had on its upkeep, indignantly rejecting both complaints of neglect occasionally made by visitors (over 16,000 came in 1955) and suggestions that the castle should be entrusted to the Ministry of Works.

Eventually the burden proved too great, and in 1986 Jewell reached an agreement with English Heritage under which Stokesay was placed in the guardianship of that body, and would become its property following her own death (which occurred in 1992). By this time the castle was in a state 'not … of abject decay and absolute neglect, but … rather starved and worn out'.

A four-year campaign of restoration followed, intended to be as unobtrusive in its impact as the works carried out by John Derby Allcroft a century earlier. Its success may be judged to the extent to which Stokesay Castle looks now, as it has probably always looked, a permanent feature of the surrounding landscape.